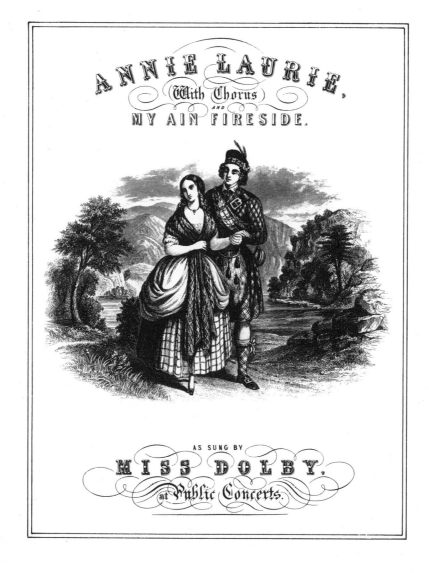

ANNIE LAURIE,
With Chorus
AND
MY AIN FIRESIDE.

AS SUNG BY
MISS DOLBY,
at Public Concerts.

THROWING THE HAMMER.

A Song of Scotland

Contents

Cover design – Howard Brown

Wise Publications
Music Sales Limited, 78 Newman Street, London W1P 3LA

ROTHESAY BAY

TRADITIONAL

PIANO

Andante affettuoso

Fu' yel-low lie the corn-rigs Far

down the braid hill - side; It is the braw-est har'st field A-

-lang the shores o' Clyde, And I'm a puir har'st las-sie Wha

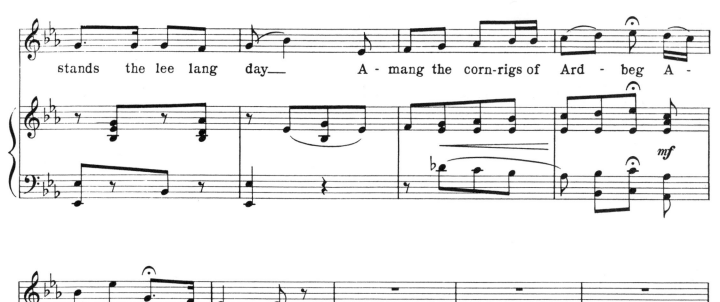

stands the lee lang day___ A - mang the corn-rigs of Ard - beg A -

- boon sweet Rothe-say Bay___

O I had ance a true love, Now, I hae nane a -

- va;___ And I had three braw bri - thers, But I hae tint them

4

a'; My Fa - ther and my Mi-ther Sleep i' the mools this

day.__ I sit my lane a-mang the rigs A - boon sweet Rothe - say

Bay__ It's a bon - nie bay at

mor - ning, And bon - nier at the Noon, But bon - niest when the

wee tear blin's my e'e,— And I think of that far Coun - trie Wha

I wad like to be. But I rise con - tent i' the morn - ing To

wark while wark I may— I' the yellow har'st field of Ard - beg A -

- boon sweet Rothe - say Bay.—

THE HUNDRED PIPERS

TRADITIONAL

a', and a' oh it's owre the Bor-der a - wa', a wa', It's
loud and clear. Will they a' re-turn to their ain deer glen? Will they

F   B♭ F   Dm

owre the Bor-der, a - wa' a - wa' we'll on and we'll march to
a' re-turn our High-land men? Sec-ond sicht-ed San-dy

F   G7   C7(sus4)   C7   F

Car - lisle Ha' wi' it's yetts, its cas-tle an' a', an' a', Wi' a
looked fu' wae an' mi - thers grat when they marched a-way

B♭   Bdim   F   C7   F   B♭ F

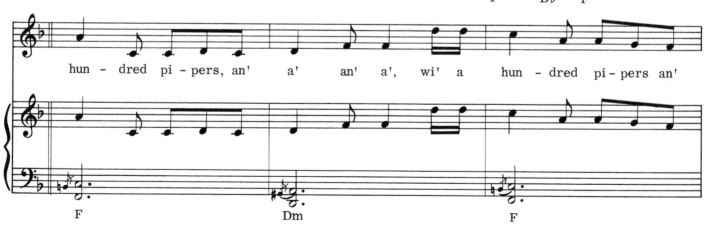

hun - dred pi -pers, an' a' an a', wi' a hun dred pi -pers an'

F   Dm   F

a', an' a', we'll__ up and gie them a blaw, a blaw, Wi a

1-2 hun — dred pi - pers an' a', an' a'. (2) Oh oor **LAST** a', an' a'.

C7

F F7 Bb Bdim

F C7 F Bb F F Bb F

3. The esk was swollen sae red and sae deep,
   But shoulder to shoulder, the brave lads kept;
   Two thousand swam owre the fall English ground.
   An' danced themselves dry to the pibroch's sound.

4. Dumfounder'd the English saw, they saw,
   Dumfounder'd, they heard the blaw, the blaw;
   Dumfounder'd, they a' raw awa' awa',
   Frae the hundred pipers an' a', an' a'.

   Wi a hundred pipers etc.

MY LOVE IS LIKE A RED RED ROSE

TRADITIONAL

My love is like a red, red rose that's
A' the seas gang dry, my dear, and the

new-ly sprung in June, My love is like a mel-o-dy that's
rocks meet with the sun, And I will love thee still, my dear, while the

sweet-ly played in tune. As fair art thou, my bon-nie lass, so
sands of life shall run. But fair-thee-well my on-ly love! oh

ANNIE LAURIE

TRADITIONAL

me her prom - ise true   Gave me her prom - ise true,   which
e'er the sun shone on   That e'er the sun shone on,   and
voice is low and sweet   Her voice is low and sweet,   and she's

Db   Eb9 Ab7   D6   Ab13 Db   Ebm7   Db   Ab13
(ped Db)

ne'er for-got will be;
dark blue is her e'e;   And for bon - nie bon-nie An-nie
a' the world to me;

Bbm   Ebm   F   Gb   Gdim

1 - 2   **3**

Laur- ie   I'd lay__ me doon and dee. (2) her__ dee.
(3) like__

Db   F   Bbm   Eb9 Ab7   Db   Ab13   Db

LOCH LOMOND

Poco lento

TRADITIONAL

3. The wee birdies sing, and the wild flowers spring,
    While in sunshine the waters are sleepin',
    But the broken heart it kens nae second spring again,
    Tho' the waefu' may cease frae their greetin'
        Oh you tak' the high road etc.,

BONNIE DUNDEE

TRADITIONAL

fill up my can, Come sad-dle my hor-ses, and call out my men; Un-

hook the West Port, and let us gae free, For it's

up wi' the bon-nets o' Bon-nie Dun-dee. (2) Dun- Bon-nie Dun-dee.

1-3 / **LAST**

3. There are hills beyond Pentland, and hills beyond Forth,
   Be there lords in the south, there are chiefs in the north;
   There are brave duinnewassels, three thousand times three
   Will cry "Hey for the bonnets o' bonnie dundee".
   (To Chorus)

4. The awa' to the hills, to the lea, to the rocks,
   Ere I own a usurper, I'll crouch wi' the fox;
   And tremble, false whigs, in the midst o' your glee,
   Ye hae no seen the last o' my bonnets an' me.
   (To Chorus)

BONNIE MARY OF ARGYLE

TRADITIONAL

TEMPO 120

This arrangement © Copyright 1972 by
DORSEY BROS. MUSIC LTD., 78 Newman Street, London, W1P 3LA

AULD LANG SYNE

TRADITIONAL

SCOTLAND THE BRAVE

Arranged by
EDMUNDO ROS & RONALD HANMER

WEE COOPER O' FIFE

TRADITIONAL

Allegro

There was a wee Coo-per who lived__ in Fife,
Wad — na bake, nor she wad — na brew,

Nick— e -ty, Nack— e -ty, noo, noo, noo, and he has got— ten a
Nick— e -ty, Nack— e -ty, noo, noo, noo, for the spoil— ing o' her

gen— tle wife,
come— ly hue,

Hey Wil— ly Wal— lack— y, hoo John Dou— gal, a

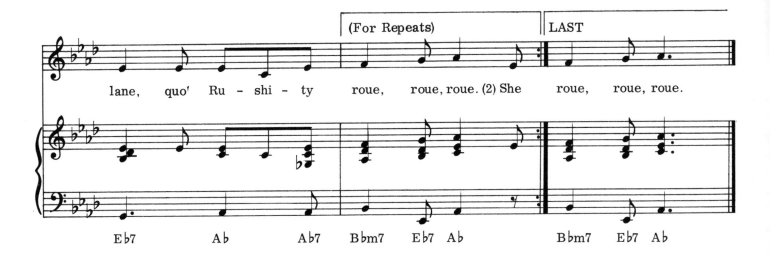

(For Repeats)   LAST

lane,   quo' Ru — shi — ty   roue,   roue, roue. (2) She   roue,   roue, roue.

Eb7   Ab   Ab7   Bbm7   Eb7 Ab   Bbm7   Eb7 Ab

3. She wadna card, nor she wadna spin,
    Nickety, Nackety, noo, noo, noo,
For the shamin' o' her gentle kin'
    Hey Willy Wallacky, hoo John Dougal,
    Alane, quo' Rushity, roue, roue, roue.

4. She wadna wash, nor she wadna wring,
    Nickety, Nackety, noo, noo, noo,
For the spoilin' o' her gowden ring,
    Hey Willy Wallacky, hoo John Dougal,
    Alane, quo' Rushity, roue, roue, roue.

5. The Cooper has gane to his woo' pack,
    Nickety, Nackety, noo, noo, noo,
And he's laid a sheep's skin on his wife's back,
    Hey Willy Wallacky, hoo John Dougal,
    Alane, quo' Rushity, roue, roue, roue.

6. It's I'll no thrash ye for your gentle kin,
    Nickety, Nackety, noo, noo, noo,
But I will thrash my ain sheep's skin,
    Hey Willy Wallacky, hoo John Dougal,
    Alane, quo' Rushity, roue, roue, roue.

7. O I will bake, and I will brew,
    Nickety, Nackety, noo, noo, noo,
And nae mair think o' my comely hue,
    Hey Willy Wallacky, hoo John Dougal,
    Alane, quo' Rushity, roue, roue, roue.

8. O I will card, and I will spin,
    Nickety, Nackety, noo, noo, noo,
And nae mair think o' my gentle kin,
    Hey Willy Wallacky, hoo John Dougal,
    Alane, quo' Rushity, roue, roue, roue.

9. O I will wash, and I will wring,
    Nickety, Nackety, noo, noo, noo,
And nae mair think o' my gowden ring,
    Hey Willy Wallacky, hoo John Dougal,
    Alane, quo' Rushity, roue, roue, roue.

Moral:-

10. A' ye wha ha'e gotten a gentle wife,
    Nickety, Nackety, noo, noo, noo,
Just you send for the wee cooper o' Fife,
    Hey Willy Wallacky, hoo John Dougal,
    Alane, quo' Rushity, roue, roue, roue.

THE BALINTORE FISHERMAN
Polka

JAMES BLUE

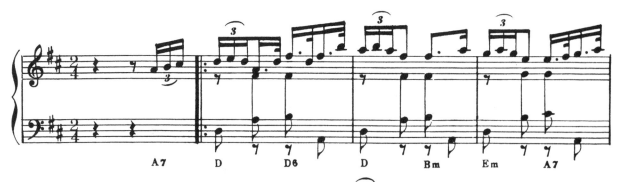

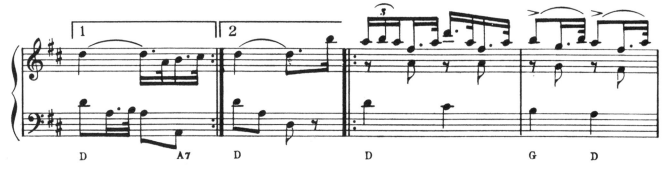

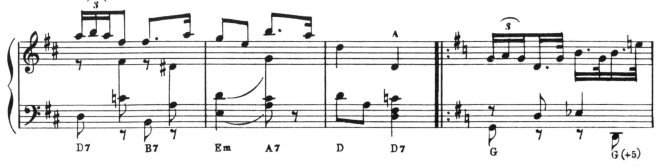

DOWN IN THE GLEN

Words and Music by
HARRY GORDON & TOMMIE CONNOR

Twi - light is soft - ly fall - ing as the sun sinks in the West, The
one I love is call - ing, "Shep - herd, come home to rest."

REFRAIN

At hush of ev - en - tide O'er the hills be - yond the Clyde I go roam - ing to my

THE TARTAN

Words by
SYDNEY BELL

Music by
KENNETH McKELLAR

Quick March (*Swing the Tartan brightly*)

VERSE

1. There are hun-dreds of tar-tans so love-ly to see, And ma-ny a
2. The Mac-ken-zie(5) is not-ed, the Lind-say is grand, The Gor-don's fa-
3. There's the Bruce, the Bu-chan-an,(7) the Fra-ser and Mac-Bean,(8) Mac-Don-ald, Mac-
4. Aye!(10) the chil-dren of Sco-tia(11) may roam the world o'er But their thoughts aye(12) re-

fa-mous has graced the bare knee; And the sett(1) that I wear is both
-mi-liar in ma-ny a land; And the Ca-me-ron men have a
-mil-lan, Mac-pher-son and Mac-Lean;(9) But I can't name them all and it's
-turn to the land they a-dore, And the skirl o' the pipes sends the

GLOSSARY

1 Sett — tartan pattern.	5 MacKenzie — (pronounce Makinzie)	9 MacLean — pronounce MaCleen.
2 Braw (rhyme with "law") — handsome.	6 MacLeod — (pronounce MaCloud)	10 Aye! (rhyme with "my") — Yes!
3 a' (simply the vowel sound in the word) — all.	7 Buchanan — (pronounce Bukanan)	11 Scotia (pronounce Skosha) Scotland.
4 Hielands (pronounced Heelands) — Highlands.	8 MacBean — (pronounce MacBeen)	12 Aye (rhyme with "my") — ever.

an - cient and braw,(2) It's the pride o' my heart and the dear-est of a'.(3)
right to be proud, With the Camp-bells and Stew - arts, Mac-Leod(6) of Mac - Leod.
no use to try, So I give you "The Tar - tan from Sol - way to Skye!"
heart beat-ing high, And the Tar - tans of home bring a tear to the eye.

C   Gdim   G   Ddim   C6sus   D7

CHORUS

Then it's Hey! for THE TAR-TAN and Ho! for THE TAR-TAN! The stamp o' the

mp - mf

G   D7   G

Hie-lands(4) from Skye to Dun-dee; And it's proud I am bear-ing THE TAR - TAN I'm

A7   D7   G   D7

1 for Repeat Chos. only   2. 3. 4th Verses   Last time

wear-ing, The pride o' my Clan and THE TAR-TAN for me! Then it's me! (2) The Mac- me!
(3) There's the
(4) Aye! the

D.S.

Fine

G   C   G   D7 G   D7   G   D7   G

A GORDON FOR ME (The Pride of Them All)

Words and Music by
ROBERT WILSON

With a lilt

1. I'm Geor - gie Mac Kay of the H. - L. - I. I'm fond of the lass-ies and a drap-pie for-bye, One day when out walk-ing I chanced to see, A bon-nie wee lass wi' a glint in her ee' *(eye)* Says I to the lass-ie will you walk for a

2. I Court - ed that girl on the banks of the Dee, I made up my mind she was fash-ioned for me, Soon I was a' think-ing how nice it would be If she would con--sent to get mar-ried to me. The day we were wed, the grass was so

OLD SCOTCH MOTHER MINE

Words and Music by
RAY McKAY & JOSEPH MAXWELL

REFRAIN

Old Scotch Mo - ther Mine____ You are with me all the while____ Your

kind old eyes____ And your dear sweet smile____

Tho' we're far a - part____ For the sake of Auld Lang Syne____ God

bless and keep you Old Scotch Mo - ther Mine.____ Mine.____

TOBERMORY BAY

Words and Music by
JOHNNY REINE, KENNETH NORTH
& JIMMY HARPER

fish - ing boats, the nip of Au - tumn wea - ther, ___ The spind-rift, the ex - cite - ment of the
kind - ly folk too hon - est to de - ceive me, ___ I'd guar - an - tee their good-ness an - y

Db   Ab   Fm   Bb7

fray,   The toil of haul - ing in the nets to - geth - er, ___ Then
day   Their High-land hearts are tru - er gold be - lieve me, ___ Than

Eb7 Bbm7   Eb7   Ab   Ab+   Db

hom - ing back to Tob - er - mor - y   Bay. ___
all the gold in Tob - er - mor - y   Bay. ___

Eb7   Ab   Bbm7 Ab   Fm   Cm

|1   ‖2

2. Down   3. The birds need on - ly lift their wings and wan - der, ___ I

Db   Eb7   Db   Eb7   Ab   Ab+   Db

THE DARK ISLAND

Words by DAVID SILVER

Music by IAIN MACLACHLAN

VERSE

-way to the west - ward I'm long - ing to be, Where the

beaut - ies of hea - ven un - fold by the sea; Where the

sweet purp -le heath - er blooms frag - rant and free, On a

hill - top high a - bove the dark — is — — — land. Oh—

G   Am7   D7   G   G

CHORUS

isle of my child - hood I'm dream-ing of thee, As the steam - er leaves

G   G   C   G   G

Ob- an   and pass - es Ti - ree; Soon I'll cap - ture the mag - ic that

G   G   Am7 D7 Am   Em

ling - ers for me, When I'm back once more up - on the dark—

C   G   G   Am7   D7

2. So gentle the sea breeze,
   That ripples the bay,
   Where the stream joins the ocean,
   And young children play;
   On the strand of pure silver,
   I'll welcome each day,
   And I'll roam for ever more,
   The Dark island.

3. True gem of the Hebrides,
   Bathed in the light,
   Of the mid-summer dawning,
   That follows the night;
   How I yearn for the cries,
   Of the seagulls in flight,
   As they circle high above,
   The Dark island.

BLUEBELL POLKA

Words by
PADDY ROBERTS

Music by
F. STANLEY

AN ERISKAY LOVE LILT

Gradh Geal mo chridh

Sung by Mary Macinnes, Eriskay
Last three verses by KENNETH MACLEOD

English adaptation and pianoforte accompaniment by
MARJORY KENNEDY-FRASER

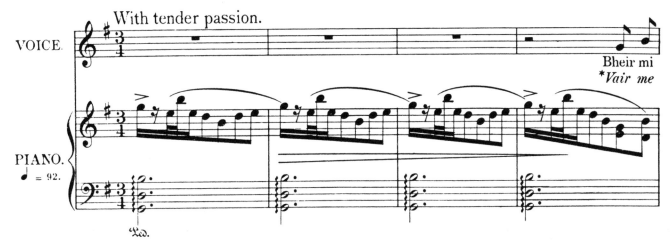

oidh - che fliuch is fuar   Ghabh mi cuairt   is mi leam fhin,   Gus an
lone - ly dear white heart   *Black the night   or wild the sea,*   *By love's*
siar   air agh-aidh cuain   'Se   mo dhuan - sa Cruit-mo-chridh,   Guth mo

d'rain - ig mi'n t-àit   Fai'n robh gradh   geal mo   chridh.   Bheir mi
light   my foot   finds   The old path - way to   thee.   *Vair me*
luaidh   anns gach stuaidh   'Ga mo nuall - an   gu   tir.

o   ro bhan o   Bheir mi o   ro bhan i   Bheir mi o   ru   o
o   ro van o   Vair me o   ro van ee   Vair me   o   ru   o

ho   'S mi tha bròn - ach's tu'm   dhith.
ho   Sad am I   with-out   thee.

'Na mo chlàr-saich cha robh ceòl 'Na mo mheoir-ean cha robh àgh, Rinn do
Thou'rt the mus - ic of my heart, Harp of joy, oh cruit mo chridh, Moon of
Gur tu m'òig - e is mo rùn, Mo re-iùil thu anns an oidhch, Tha mo

phòg - sa mo leon, Fhuair mi Eol - as an dàin. Bheir mi o ro bhan
guid - ance by night, Strength and light thou'rt to me. Vair me o ro van
dhrùidh - eachd ad shùil, Tha mo chiurr-adh ad loinn.

o Bheir mi o ro bhan i Bheir mi o ru o ho 'S mi tha
o Vair me o ro van ee Vair me o ru o ho Sad am

bron - ach 's tu 'm dhith. _____
I with-out thee. _____

* "Harp of my heart!" pronounced "crootch mo chree!"

THE DUNDEE GHOST

Words and Music by
MATT McGINN

dead man sel-dom walks, he ver-y rare-ly talks,—It's not ver-y of-ten you'll
rea-son I a-rose was to get my-self some clothes,—For it real-ly gets heck of a

find him run-nin' a-roon!___ But I am a ref-u-gee fae a
cold be-low_ the grun!___ But I whispered to my-self, ach, I

grave-yard in Dun-dee, And I've come to haunt some hoo-ses in Glas-gow toon___
think I might as well hang a-roond for a while_and hae some fun___

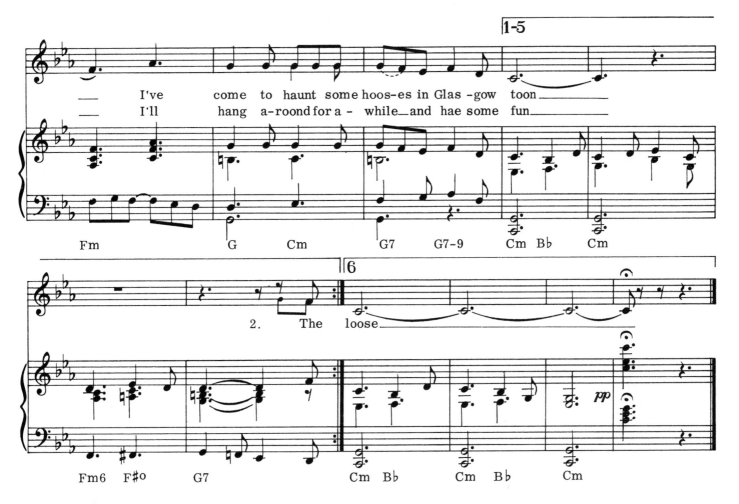

I've come to haunt some hoos-es in Glas-gow toon
I'll hang a-round for a - while and hae some fun

Fm G Cm G7 G7-9 Cm Bb Cm

2. The loose

Fm6 F#o G7 Cm Bb Cm Bb Cm

3. A man put oot his light on a cold a wintry night,
I showed him one of my eyes and slapped his head;
He says, "Oh!" and I says "Boo!"
He says, "Who the hell are you?"
I says, "Don't be feart I'm only a man that's dead.
Oh, don't be feart I'm only a man that's dead."

4. Now the fella knelt and prayed and this was what he said;
"Why in the name of God have you picked on me?"
So I pulled away his rug
And I scalped him on the lug,
"The reason," I says, "Is just to let you see,"
"The reason," I says, "Is just to let you see."

5. When he brought the police in, I battered them on the chin,
The police turned around and he blamed my friend,
He marched him to the jail
And he'll be in there quite a while,
But I'll see naebody takes a single end;
But I'll see naebody takes a single end.

6. The police thought "I'm daft," and a lot of people laughed,
When the fella said a ghost was in his hoose,
But what the fella said was true
And I might be visitin' you,
So just remember I'm still on the loose,
So just remember I'm still on the loose.

THE RED YO-YO

Words and Music by
MATT McGINN

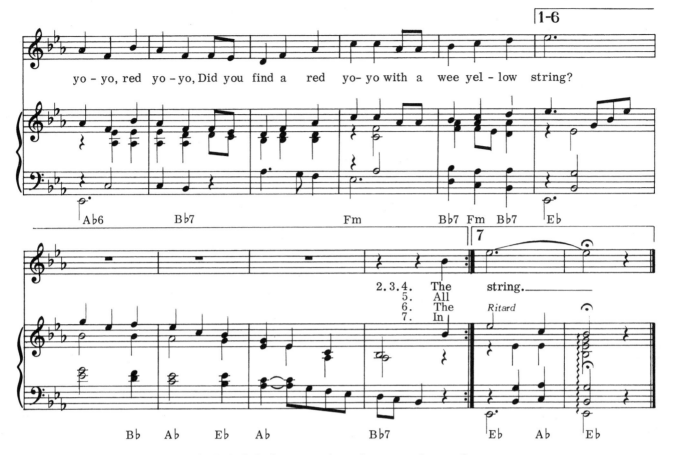

yo - yo, red yo-yo, Did you find a red yo-yo with a wee yel - low string?

Ab6   Bb7   Fm   Bb7 Fm Bb7 Eb

2.3.4. The   string.
5.   All
6.   The   *Ritard*
7.   In

Bb   Ab   Eb   Ab   Bb7   Eb   Ab   Eb

3. The kids left their pencils and paper and stencils
   To knock on the doors all around,
   And as they were rapping and ringing and clapping
   They asked all the folk of the town.
   (Chorus)

4. The policemen soon learned and they were concerned,
   They left other cases aside;
   The whole of the force was alerted, of course,
   And they went on the T.V. and cried:
   (Chorus)

5. All over the country the common and gentry
   Were watching their wee T.V. screen;
   Things really got goin', son, when President Johnson
   Received an appeal from the Queen.
   (Chorus)

6. The wires were tremblin' when he phoned the Kremlin
   To ask about Annie's yo-yo,
   But they soon agreed with the greatest of speed
   To raise it before the U.N.O.
   (Chorus)

7. In Peking and Paris and way up in Harris
   They were searching in vain, high and low,
   When suddenly Annie announced that her Granny
   Had bought her another yo-yo.
   (Chorus)

FINAL CHORUS:
   And it was a red yo-yo, red yo-yo ... etc.

ON THE BANKS OF ALLAN WATER

TRADITIONAL

sought her, and a win - ning tongue had he;____ On the banks of Al -lan
brought her, and the sol - dier false was he;____ On the banks of Al -lan

Wa - ter none so gay as she.
Wa - ter none so sad as she.

2. On the she

3. On the banks of Allan Water,
   When the winter snow fell fast,
   Still was seen the miller's daughter;
   Chilling blew the blast.
   But the miller's lovely daughter
   Both from cold and care was free.
   On the banks of Allan Water
   There a corpse lay she.

THE PIPER OF DUNDEE

TRADITIONAL

It's some gat swords and some gat nane,
And some were dancing mad their lane,
And mony a vow o'weir was ta'en
That night at Amulrie.
There was Tullibardine and Burleigh
And Struan, Keith and Ogilvie,
And brave Carnegie, wha but he,
The Piper o' Dundee.

LEEZIE LINDSAY

TRADITIONAL

3. "O Leezie, lass, ye maun ken little,
   If sae ye dinna ken me;
   For my name is Lord Ronald Mac Donald,
   A chieftain o' high degree".

4. "She has kilted her coats o' green satin,
   She has kilted them up to the knee;
   An' she's off wi' Lord Ronald Mac Donald,
   His bride and his darling to be".

CA' THE YOWES

TRADITIONAL

This arrangement © Copyright 1972 by
DORSEY BROS. MUSIC LTD., 78 Newman Street, London, W1P 3LA

THE FLOWERS O' THE FOREST

TRADITIONAL

Lento (with expression)

I've heard the lilt - in'___ at the ewe___ milk - in',

F   Gm7   C   Dm   Am   F   Gm   Gm7   C7

lass - es a lilt - in' be - fore___ dawn of day.

F   Gm7   C   Dm   Am   F   C(sus4)   F

Now___ there's a moan - in' on Il - ka Green___ loan - in' the

Cm7   F7   B♭maj7   Bdim   C7(sus4) C7 Dm   C   Gm7   C7

flow'rs of the for — est are a' wede a — wa'.

F   B♭   F   Am7   Gm7   C9   F

2.   At bughts in the mornin', nae blithe lads are scornin',
     Lassies are lanely, an' dowie, an' wae,
     Nae daffin', nae gabbin', but sighin' an' sabbin';
     Ilk ane lifts her laglin', an' hies her awa'.

3.   We'll ha'e nae mair liltin' at the ewe milkin',
     Women an' bairns are heartless an' wae;
     Sighin' an' moanin' on Ilka Green loanin',
     The flowers o' the forest are a' wede awa'.

MY AIN FOLK

Words by
WILFRID MILLS

Music by
LAURA G. LEMON

Simply and pathetically.

Far frae my hame I wan_der; But still my thoughts re _ turn To my ain folk ower yonder, In the sheil_ing by the burn. I see the co_sy in_gle, And the mist a_bune the brae: And

più mosso.

O' their ab-sent ane they're tell-ing— The auld folk by the fire: And I mark the swift tears well-ing, As the rud-dy flame leaps high'r. How the mi-ther wad ca-ress me Were I but by her side: Now she prays that Heav'n will bless me, Tho' the

A bon-nie lass is greet-ing, Tho' she

strives to stay the tears:— Ah! sweet will be our meet-ing Af-ter

mon-y wea-ry years. Soon my fond arms shall en-fold ye, As I

ca' you ev-er mine— Still a-bides the love I told ye In the

BONNIE WEE THING

TRADITIONAL

Bon - nie wee thing, can - nie wee thing, love - ly wee thing, wert thou mine,

I wad wear thee in my bos - om lest my je - wel it should tine.

Wish ful - ly I look and lan - guish in that bon - nie
Wit, and grace, and love and beau - ty, in ae con - stel -

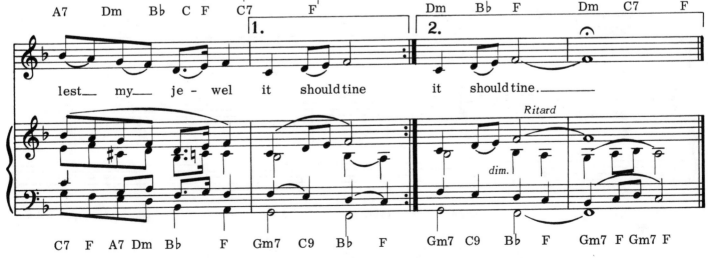

WILL YE NO COME BACK AGAIN

TRADITIONAL

CHORUS

MY HEART'S IN THE HIGHLANDS

Slowly

TRADITIONAL

AFTON WATER

TRADITIONAL

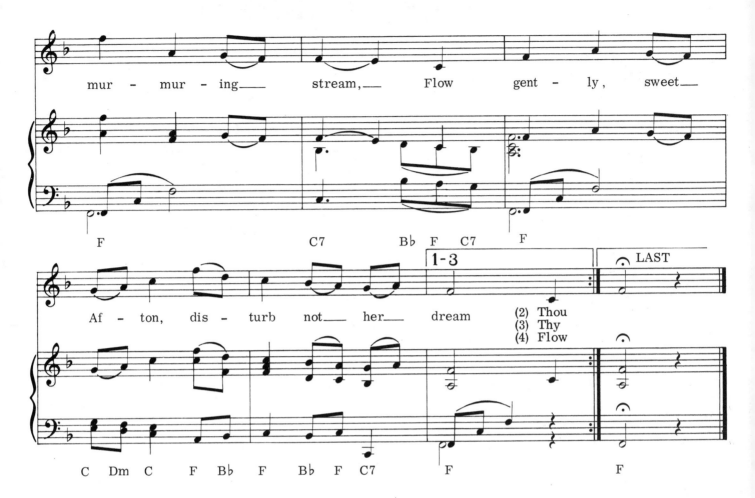

mur - mur - ing___ stream,___ Flow gent - ly, sweet___

F   C7   B♭ F C7   F

1-3   **LAST**

Af - ton, dis - turb not___ her___ dream
(2) Thou
(3) Thy
(4) Flow

C Dm C F B♭ F B♭ F C7   F   F

2. Thou stock dove whose echo resounds thro' the glen,
   Ye wild whistling blackbirds in yon thorny den,
   Thou green crested lap wing, thy screaming for bear,
   I charge you disturb not my slumbering fair.

3. Thy crystal stream Afton, how lovely it glides
   And winds by the cot where my Mary resides!
   How wanton thy waters her snowy feet lave
   As, gath'ring sweet flow'rets she stems thy clear wave.

4. Flow gently, sweet Afton among thy green braes,
   Flow gently, sweet river, the theme of my lays:
   My Mary's asleep by thy murmuring stream,
   Flow gently, sweet Afton, disturb not her dream.

THE ROAD TO THE ISLES

Words by
KENNETH MACLEOD

To an air played by MALCOLM JOHNSON, Barra,
on the chanter; arranged for Voice and Harp,
(or Piano) by
PATUFFA KENNEDY-FRASER

Tummel and Loch Rannoch and Loch-a-ber I will go, By heather tracks wi' heaven in their
wiles; If it's think-in' in your in-ner heart braggart's in my step, You've
or (swank is)
ne-ver smelt the tan-gle o' the Isles. Oh, the far Cool-ins are
D.S.
1st. & 2nd. Verses.
3rd. Verse.
put-tin' love on me, As step I wi' my cromak to the Isles. It's by Isles.
It's the
Fine.

Reproduced and printed by
Halstan & Co. Ltd., Amersham, Bucks.